1979 U.K.

YEARBOOK

ISBN: 9781793045126

This book gives a fascinating and informative insight into life in the United Kingdom in 1979. It includes everything from the most popular music of the year to the cost of a buying a new house. Additionally, there are chapters covering people in high office, the best-selling films of the year and all the main news and events. Want to know which team won the FA Cup or which British personalities were born in 1979? All this and much more awaits you within.

© Liberty Eagle Publishing Ltd. 2018
All Rights Reserved

INDEX

FIRST EDITION

1979

January
M	T	W	T	F	S	S
1	2	3	4	5	6	7
8	9	10	11	12	13	14
15	16	17	18	19	20	21
22	23	24	25	26	27	28
29	30	31				

◑:5 ○:13 ◐:21 ●:28

February
M	T	W	T	F	S	S
			1	2	3	4
5	6	7	8	9	10	11
12	13	14	15	16	17	18
19	20	21	22	23	24	25
26	27	28				

◑:4 ○:12 ◐:20 ●:26

March
M	T	W	T	F	S	S
			1	2	3	4
5	6	7	8	9	10	11
12	13	14	15	16	17	18
19	20	21	22	23	24	25
26	27	28	29	30	31	

◑:5 ○:13 ◐:21 ●:28

April
M	T	W	T	F	S	S
						1
2	3	4	5	6	7	8
9	10	11	12	13	14	15
16	17	18	19	20	21	22
23	24	25	26	27	28	29
30						

◑:4 ○:12 ◐:19 ●:26

May
M	T	W	T	F	S	S
	1	2	3	4	5	6
7	8	9	10	11	12	13
14	15	16	17	18	19	20
21	22	23	24	25	26	27
28	29	30	31			

◑:4 ○:12 ◐:19 ●:26

June
M	T	W	T	F	S	S
				1	2	3
4	5	6	7	8	9	10
11	12	13	14	15	16	17
18	19	20	21	22	23	24
25	26	27	28	29	30	

◑:2 ○:10 ◐:17 ●:24

July
M	T	W	T	F	S	S
						1
2	3	4	5	6	7	8
9	10	11	12	13	14	15
16	17	18	19	20	21	22
23	24	25	26	27	28	29
30	31					

◑:2 ○:9 ◐:16 ●:24

August
M	T	W	T	F	S	S
		1	2	3	4	5
6	7	8	9	10	11	12
13	14	15	16	17	18	19
20	21	22	23	24	25	26
27	28	29	30	31		

◑:1 ○:8 ◐:14 ●:22 ◑:30

September
M	T	W	T	F	S	S
					1	2
3	4	5	6	7	8	9
10	11	12	13	14	15	16
17	18	19	20	21	22	23
24	25	26	27	28	29	30

○:6 ◐:13 ●:21 ◑:29

October
M	T	W	T	F	S	S
1	2	3	4	5	6	7
8	9	10	11	12	13	14
15	16	17	18	19	20	21
22	23	24	25	26	27	28
29	30	31				

○:5 ◐:12 ●:21 ◑:28

November
M	T	W	T	F	S	S
			1	2	3	4
5	6	7	8	9	10	11
12	13	14	15	16	17	18
19	20	21	22	23	24	25
26	27	28	29	30		

○:4 ◐:11 ●:19 ◑:26

December
M	T	W	T	F	S	S
					1	2
3	4	5	6	7	8	9
10	11	12	13	14	15	16
17	18	19	20	21	22	23
24	25	26	27	28	29	30
31						

○:3 ◐:11 ●:19 ◑:26

PEOPLE IN HIGH OFFICE

Monarch - Queen Elizabeth II
Reign: 6th February 1952 - Present
Predecessor: King George VI
Heir Apparent: Charles, Prince of Wales

Prime Minister

James Callaghan - Labour
5th April 1976 - 4th May 1979

Margaret Thatcher - Conservative
4th May 1979 - 28th November 1990

Australia

Canada

United States

Prime Minister
Malcom Fraser
Liberal Party
11th November 1975 -
11th March 1983

Prime Minister
Pierre Trudeau
Liberal Party
20th April 1968 -
4th June 1979

President
Jimmy Carter
Democratic Party
20th January 1977 -
20th January 1981

Brazil

President
Ernesto Geisel (1974-1979)
João Figueiredo (1979-1985)

Cuba

President
Fidel Castro (1976-2008)

China

Communist Party Leader
Hua Guofeng (1976-1981)

France

President
Valéry Giscard d'Estaing (1974-1981)

India

Prime Minister
Morarji Desai (1977-1979)
Charan Singh (1979-1980)

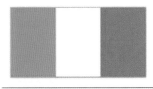

Ireland

Prime Minister
Jack Lynch (1977-1979)
Charles Haughey (1979-1981)

Israel

Prime Minister
Menachem Begin (1977-1983)

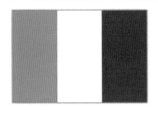

Italy

Prime Minister
Giulio Andreotti (1976-1979)
Francesco Cossiga (1979-1980)

 Japan

Prime Minister
Masayoshi Ōhira (1978-1980)

 New Zealand

Prime Minister
Robert Muldoon (1975-1984)

 Pakistan

President
Muhammad Zia-ul-Haq (1978-1988)

 South Africa

Prime Minister
P. W. Botha (1978-1984)

 Soviet Union

Communist Party Leader
Leonid Brezhnev (1964-1982)

 Spain

Prime Minister
Adolfo Suárez (1976-1981)

 Turkey

Prime Minister
Bülent Ecevit (1978-1979)
Süleyman Demirel (1979-1980)

 West Germany

Chancellor
Helmut Schmidt (1974-1982)

BRITISH NEWS & EVENTS

JAN

1st | French carmaker Peugeot completes its takeover of the European division of financially troubled American carmaker Chrysler; this was agreed in 1978 and includes the British operations of the former Rootes Group.

3rd | An unofficial strike of all Transport and General Workers' Union (TGWU) lorry drivers begins with petrol distribution held up and petrol stations closed across the country. The strikes were made official on the 11th January by the TGWU and 12th January by the United Road Transport Union. With 80% of the nation's goods transported by road essential supplies were put in danger as striking drivers picketed those firms that continued to work. More than 1,000,000 UK workers were laid off temporarily during the disputes.

6th | The Village People's Y.M.C.A becomes their only UK No.1 single. *Fun Fact: At its peak it sold over 150,000 copies a day and is one of fewer than 40 singles to have sold at least 10 million physical copies worldwide.*

10th | Prime Minister James Callaghan returns from economic conference in Guadeloupe in the West Indies to a Britain in a state of industrial unrest. Asked how he was going to deal with the problem he replies with the comment, "I don't think other people in the world would share the view [that] there is mounting chaos." The Sun newspaper reports his comments with the famous headline: "Crisis? What Crisis?" These three words have since been attributed to helping bring down the Labour government and have become part of political folklore.

15th | Rail workers begin a 24-hour strike.

22nd January: Tens of thousands of public-workers, including gravediggers, hospital staff, school caretakers, airport staff, and waste collectors, go on strike in what becomes known as the "Winter of Discontent". This was the biggest individual day of strike action since the General Strike of 1926.

JAN

29th	Lorry drivers in the south west accept a pay deal, awarded by an Arbitration Panel, of a rise of up to 20%, just £1 per week less than the union had been striking for; this settlement proved a model which would be accepted throughout the country.

FEB

1st	Gravediggers call off a strike in Liverpool. A Department of Environment note shows that at the height of the dispute there were 150 unburied bodies stored in a factory in Speke, with 25 more being added every day.
2nd	Sid Vicious, the former Sex Pistols guitarist, is found dead in New York after apparently suffocating on his own vomit as a result of a heroin overdose. 21-year-old London-born Vicious (real name John Simon Ritchie) was on bail for the second-degree murder of his girlfriend Nancy Spungen, who was found stabbed to death in their Chelsea Hotel room three months earlier.
9th	Trevor Francis signs for Nottingham Forest from Birmingham City in British football's first £1 million deal.
14th	The "Saint Valentine's Day Concordat" between Trades Union Congress and Government marks the beginning of the end to the Winter of Discontent. *In total in 1979, 29,474,000 working days would be lost to industrial disputes, compared with 9,306,000 in 1978.*
15th	Opinion polls show the Conservatives up to 20 points ahead of Labour - Labour's popularity had slumped dramatically due to the fallout from the recent industrial unrest.
22nd	Saint Lucia gains its independence from the United Kingdom.

MAR

1st	Scottish devolution referendum: Scotland votes by a majority of 77,437 for a Scottish Assembly. This is not implemented due to a condition that at least 40% of the electorate must support the proposal (with a turnout of 64% this represented only 32.9% of the registered electorate).
1st	Welsh devolution referendum: Wales votes against devolution with only 12% of the Welsh electorate voting in favour of establishing an assembly.
1st	Conservative candidate David Waddington is returned to Parliament in the Clitheroe by-election.
17th	Nottingham Forest beat Southampton 3-2 at Wembley in front of 96,952 supporters to win the Football League Cup for the second year running.
17th	The Penmanshiel Tunnel (constructed 1845-1846) in Berwickshire, Scotland, collapses during engineering works killing two workers. It is later determined that the ground is not stable enough to excavate and rebuild the tunnel, so it is sealed up and a new alignment made for the railway.
18th	An explosion believed to be caused by a build-up of methane gas at the Golborne colliery near Wigan in Lancashire kills three men.
22nd	Sir Richard Sykes, the British ambassador to the Netherlands, is assassinated by the Provisional Irish Republican Army (PIRA) in The Hague.
28th	James Callaghan's government loses a motion of confidence by one vote forcing a General Election.

29th	James Callaghan announces that the General Election will be held on the 3rd May. All of the major opinion polls point towards a Conservative win which would make Margaret Thatcher the first female Prime Minister of Britain.
30th	Airey Neave, the Conservative Northern Ireland spokesman, is killed by an Irish National Liberation Army bomb in the House of Commons car park. *Historical Fact: Neave was a World War Two veteran and was the first British prisoner-of-war to succeed in escaping from Oflag IV-C at Colditz Castle.*

President of Malta, Anton Buttigieg, saluting HMS London leaving the Grand Harbour.

31st March: The Royal Navy withdraws from Malta meaning that for the first time in a millennium it is no longer a military base for any foreign power. *Fun Fact: The 31st March, Freedom Day, is celebrated annually and is a Maltese national holiday.*

	Statistics show that the economy shrank by 0.8% in the first quarter of the year sparking fears that Britain could soon be faced with its second recession in four years.
4th	19-year-old bank worker Josephine Whitaker is murdered in Halifax; she is the 10th woman to be murdered by the Yorkshire Ripper.
7th	The last RT type double decker bus (RT624) runs on route 62 in London. *Fun Fact: The bus has been preserved by bus and coach operator Ensignbus, and was the last of the 4,825 RT's that had been operated by London Transport.*
23rd	New Zealand-born teacher and Anti-Nazi League protestor Blair Peach is fatally injured after being struck on the head during an anti-racism demonstration in Southall, Middlesex. A later Metropolitan Police report into his death determines that one of their own officers was probably responsible.

MAY

1st	The London Underground Jubilee line begins operating passenger services for the first time after being officially opened by the Prince of Wales.
4th	The Conservatives win the General Election with a 43-seat majority and Margaret Thatcher becomes the first female Prime Minister of the United Kingdom. Liberal Party leader Jeremy Thorpe is the most notable MP to lose his seat in the election. Despite being 67 years old and having lost the General Election James Callaghan stays on as Labour leader (replaced by Michael Foot on the 10th November 1980). Among the new members of parliament is 36-year-old MP for Huntingdon, and future Prime Minister, John Major.
8th	Former Liberal Party leader and MP Jeremy Thorpe goes on trial at the Old Bailey charged with attempted murder. Thorpe was acquitted on all charges, but the case, and the furore surrounding it, ended his political career.
12th	Arsenal defeat Manchester United 3-2 in the FA Cup final at Wembley Stadium in front of 99,219 fans.
15th	The Prices Commission, set up in under the Counter-Inflation Act 1973 in an attempt to control inflation, is abolished by the government.

21st May: Elton John becomes the first megastar to perform live in the Soviet Union. The tour consisted of eight concerts in total: four at the Great October Hall in Leningrad (now Saint Petersburg), and four more at the Rossya Hotel in Moscow. He also played a spontaneous set in a Moscow restaurant.

21st	Conservative MPs back Margaret Thatcher's proposals to sell off parts of nationalised industries; during the year the Government will begin to sell its stake in British Petroleum.
24th	Thorpe Park at Chertsey in Surrey is officially opened to the public by Lord Louis Mountbatten. Attractions at the water-based park included: The Mountbatten Pavilion (later Port Atlantis / the Dome), Model World, A WWI Aircraft Display and the Schneider Trophy Aircraft Exhibition. *Today it is one of the UK's most popular theme parks with over 1,800,000 visitors in 2017.*
25th	It is announced that the price of milk will increase more than 10% to 15 pence a pint from the beginning of June.
30th	European Cup Final: Nottingham Forest's Trevor Francis scores the only goal of the match in their 1-0 defeat of Malmö FF in Munich.

JUN

7th	European Parliament Election: The first direct election to the European Parliament sees a landslide victory for the Conservative Party which wins 60 of the 78 seats available in England, Wales and Scotland. At 32% the turnout in Britain is the lowest of the 9 EC states taking part.
12th	The new Conservative government's first budget sees chancellor Geoffrey Howe cut the standard tax rate by 3% to 30%, and sees him slashing the top rate from 83% to 60%. The government sets a long-term aim for the basic rate of 25% (achieved in 1988). Prescription charges go up from 20p to 45p.

12th June: Bryan Allen, flying the Gossamer Albatross, becomes the first person to cross the English Channel in a human-powered aircraft. He completed the crossing in 2 hours and 49 minutes to win the £100,000 Kremer Prize. The aircraft was designed and built by a team led by Dr. Paul B. MacCready, a noted American aeronautics engineer, designer, and world soaring champion.

26th	'Moonraker', the 11th James Bond film starring Roger Moore, premieres in London. The film was Bernard Lee's final appearance as M. (he died when 'For Your Eyes Only' (1981) was in pre-production).

JUL

5th	The Queen presides over the 1000th annual open-air sitting of the Isle of Man's Parliament at Tynwald.
12th	Kiribati (formerly Gilbert Islands) gains its independence from the United Kingdom.
14th	Neil Kinnock, the 37-year-old Labour MP for Islwyn in South Wales, becomes the Shadow Secretary of State for Education and Science.
17th	Athlete Sebastian Coe sets a record time for running a mile in Oslo, completing it in 3 minutes 48.95 seconds.
23rd	The government announces £4 billion worth of public spending cuts.

AUG

1st	Following the takeover of Chrysler's European division by French carmaker Peugeot, the historic Talbot marque is revived for the range of cars previously sold in Britain as Chryslers.

AUG

9th	Brighton becomes the first major resort in Britain to officially set aside part of its seafront to nudists. Following a concerted campaign by local councillor Eileen Jakes, the council agreed to set aside a 200-yard (183m) stretch of the beach solely for nude bathers.
10th	The entire ITV network in the UK is shut down by a technician's strike (Channel Television remains unaffected) - programming was not resumed until 5.38pm on the 24th October. The dispute was estimated to have cost the companies £100 million in lost revenue.
14th	A storm in the Irish Sea hits the Fastnet yacht race. Fifteen lives and dozens of yachts are lost; of the 303 starters, only 86 finished. Emergency services, naval forces, and civilian vessels from around the west side of the English Channel were summoned to aid in what became the largest ever rescue operation in peace-time.
14th	Disgraced Labour and Co-operative Party politician John Stonehouse is released from jail after serving four years of his seven-year sentence for faking his own death.
16th	The film Quadrophenia, loosely based on The Who's 1973 rock opera of the same name, premieres in London.
24th	The Ford Cortina, Britain's best-selling car, enters its fifth generation when a restyled version of the 1976 model is launched. Prices start from £3,475 for a basic 1.3-litre engined model.
27th	Lord Mountbatten of Burma, his nephew Nicholas, and a boatboy Paul Maxwell, are assassinated by a Provisional Irish Republican Army bomb while holidaying in the Republic of Ireland. The Dowager Lady Brabourne also died from her injuries the following day in hospital. Lord Mountbatten was a retired admiral, statesman, second cousin once removed to the Queen and an uncle to The Duke of Edinburgh.
27th	Warrenpoint ambush: Eighteen British soldiers are killed and six seriously injured by IRA bombs in Northern Ireland in what was the deadliest attack on the British Army during the Troubles.
30th	Francis McGirl, a 24-year-old farmer, and Thomas McMahon, a 31-year-old upholsterer, are arrested in Dublin and charged with the murder of Lord Mountbatten and the three other victims of the bombing. McMahon was eventually convicted of the murders on the 23rd November, McGirl was acquitted due to insufficient evidence.

SEP

2nd	Police discover the body of 20-year-old student Barbara Leach near Bradford city centre. The woman is the 11th murder victim of the Yorkshire Ripper.
5th	The Queen leads the mourning at a ceremonial funeral at Westminster Abbey for Lord Mountbatten.
5th	Manchester City F.C. pay a British club record fee of £1,437,500 for Wolverhampton Wanderers midfielder Steve Daley.
8th	Wolverhampton Wanderers set a new national transfer record by paying just under £1,469,000 for Aston Villa and Scotland striker Andy Gray. *Fun Fact: Todays British transfer record fee is £105,000,000 for Brazilian Philippe Coutinho who moved from Liverpool to Barcelona in January 2018.*

SEP

21st	Two RAF Hawker Siddeley Harrier jump-jets from RAF Wittering collide over Wisbech in Cambridgeshire. Both pilots eject safely but two men and a young boy are killed, and several injured, when one of the aircraft destroys 3 dwellings.
25th	Margaret Thatcher opens the new Central Milton Keynes Shopping Centre, the largest indoor shopping centre in Britain, after its final phase is completed six years after development of the huge complex first began. *Fun Fact: Today the complex is the 14th largest shopping centre in the UK with the size of 120,773 sq metres - Westfield London, in Shepherd's Bush, is now the largest covering 241,547 sq metres.*

OCT

	Statistics show a 2.3% contraction in the economy for the third quarter of the year again sparking fresh fears of a recession.
11th	Godfrey Hounsfield wins the Nobel Prize in Physiology or Medicine jointly with Allan McLeod Cormack for his part in developing the diagnostic technique of X-ray computed tomography (the CT scan).

16th October: Comedy sketch show "Not the Nine O'Clock News" debuts on BBC 2 starring Rowan Atkinson, Chris Langham, Pamela Stephenson, Griff Rhys Jones and Mel Smith. The show would run for 4 series (27 episodes) until the 8th March 1982 and is credited with bringing alternative comedy to British television.

23rd	It is announced in the House of Commons that for the first time in 40 years Britons will be free to buy and use foreign currency without any restriction.
27th	Saint Vincent and the Grenadines gains independence from the UK.
28th	Prime Minister Margaret Thatcher welcomes Chairman Hua Guofeng to Britain, the first ever visit by a Premier of the Peoples Republic of China.

NOV

	British Leyland chief executive Michael Edwardes wins the overwhelming backing of more than 100,000 of the carmaker's employees for his restructuring plans. Over the next few years this results in the closure of several plants and the loss of some 25,000 jobs.

8th	Monty Python's 'Life of Brian', directed by Terry Jones, premieres in the UK. The film tells the story of Brian Cohen (played by Graham Chapman), a young Jewish man who is born on the same day as, and next door to, Jesus Christ, and is subsequently mistaken for the Messiah.
9th	Four men are found guilty over the killing of paperboy Carl Bridgewater who had been shot dead at a farmhouse in the Staffordshire countryside 14 months previously. James Robinson and Vincent Hickey receive life sentences with a recommended minimum of 25 years for murder, Michael Hickey (also guilty of murder) receives an indefinite custodial sentence, while Patrick Molloy is guilty of manslaughter and jailed for 12 years. *Follow Up: In February 1997, after almost two decades of imprisonment, their convictions were overturned on technical grounds and the three surviving defendants were released; the fourth defendant, Patrick Molloy, died in prison two years into his sentence. Bridgewater's murder remains officially unsolved.*

Penelope Keith and Peter Bowles on set at The Manor, Cricket St Thomas, Somerset.

11th November: The last episode of the first series of the sitcom To the Manor Born on BBC1 receives 23.95 million viewers, the all-time highest figure at that time for a recorded programme in the UK. *Fun Fact: The most watched programme to date in the UK is for an episode of EastEnders (the one where Den Watts serves wife Angie with divorce papers). This was aired on Christmas day 1986 and had 30.15 million viewers.*

13th	The Times is published for the first time in nearly a year after a dispute between management and unions over staffing levels and new technology.
13th	Miners unanimously reject a 20% pay increase and threaten to go on strike until they get their desired pay rise of 65%.
15th	The government raises the Minimum Lending Rate (interest rate) to an all-time high of 17% in its attempt to combat inflation.

NOV

15th | In Parliament Sir Anthony Blunt, art advisor to the Queen, is exposed as the 4th man in Soviet spy ring. The Queen immediately strips Blunt of his knighthood and in short order he is also removed as an Honorary Fellow of Trinity College.

DEC

2nd | Six months after winning the general election a MORI opinion poll puts the Conservatives five points behind Labour (who have a 45% share of the vote).

4th | The Hastie Fire in Hull leads to the deaths of 3 brothers. That evening the police received an anonymous telephone call from which Detective Superintendent Ron Sagar and his investigators traced a number of suspects. During questioning - and to the complete surprise and horror of the police - Bruce George Peter Lee not only confessed to starting the fire but then went on to admit to starting nine more fatal fires in Hull over the previous seven years; a total of 26 people had died in the blazes. Lee was eventually convicted of 26 counts of manslaughter and was imprisoned for life in 1981 - 11 of these convictions were overturned on appeal.

10th December: 20-year-old daredevil Eddie Kidd performs a 100mph "death-defying" 80ft jump, over a 50ft sheer drop, on his 400cc motorcycle. Kidd completed the stunt before a stunned group of spectators, fans and press, at the River Blackwater at Maldon, Essex. *Career Highlights: Eddie Kidd remained a top stunt rider winning the stunt bike world championship in 1993 over Robbie Knievel, son of Evel Knievel. He also jumped the Great Wall of China at Simatai in 1993 and had parts in several films before being paralysed in an accident in 1996. He became an OBE in 2012 for his services to charity.*

11th | Lord Soames is appointed as the transitional governor of Rhodesia to oversee its move to independence.

20th | The government publishes the Housing Bill which will give council house tenants the right to buy their homes from the following year. More than 5 million households in the United Kingdom currently occupy council houses.

1. 25th January: Pope John Paul II visits the Dominican Republic on his first overseas trip as supreme pontiff.

2. 29th January: Brenda Ann Spencer opens fire at the Grover Cleveland Elementary School in San Diego, California, killing two faculty members and wounding eight students. Her response to the action, "I don't like Mondays," later inspires the Boomtown Rats to make a song of the same name.

3. 1st February: Ayatollah Khomeini returns in triumph to Iran after 14 years in exile and is welcomed by a joyous crowd estimated (by the BBC) to be of up to five million people.

4. 7th February: Pluto enters a 20-year period inside the orbit of Neptune for the first time in 230 years.

5. 20th February: In Northern Ireland eleven loyalists known as the "Shankill Butchers" are sentenced to life in prison for 19 murders; the gang was named for its late-night kidnapping, torture and murder (by throat slashing) of random Catholic civilians in Belfast.

6. 24th February: The highest price ever paid for a pig is negotiated by breeder Russ Baize in Stamford, Texas - Baize paid $42,500 for a boar named 'Glacier' (the record stood for eighteen years).

7. 1st March: Philips publicly demonstrates a prototype of an optical digital audio disc at a press conference in Eindhoven, Netherlands.

8. 25th March: The first fully functional space shuttle orbiter, Columbia, is delivered to the John F. Kennedy Space Center, to be prepared for its first launch. Columbia was originally scheduled to lift off in late 1979, however the launch date was delayed by problems with both the Space Shuttle main engine and the thermal protection system. It eventually made the first flight of the Space Shuttle program on the 12th April 1982. Over its 22 years of service it completed 27 missions before disintegrating during re-entry near the end of its 28th mission on the 1st February 2003 - the tragedy resulted in the deaths of all seven crew members.

9. 26th March: In a ceremony at the White House President Jimmy Carter witnesses President Anwar Sadat of Egypt and Prime Minister Menachem Begin of Israel sign the Egyptian-Israeli Peace Treaty.

10.	31st March: The 24th Eurovision Song Contest is held at the International Convention Centre in Jerusalem, Israel and the 19 countries taking part see Israel win for the second year running. The winning song "Hallelujah" was performed by Gali Atari and Milk and Honey.
11.	2nd April: The world's first anthrax epidemic begins in Ekaterinburg, Russia following a biological weapons plant accident. The ensuing outbreak of the disease results in approximately 100 deaths.
12.	9th April: The 51st Academy Awards honouring films released in 1978 takes place at the Dorothy Chandler Pavilion in Los Angeles. The Deer Hunter wins five awards including Best Picture, and Jon Voight and Jane Fonda win the best actor / actress awards.
13.	13th April: The longest ever doubles ping-pong match ends after 101 hours, 11 minutes and 11 seconds. The match was contested by brothers Lance, Phil, and Mark Warren, and their friend Bill Weir at Sacramento, California.
14.	17th April: Four Royal Ulster Constabulary officers are killed by a Provisional Irish Republican Army bomb in Bessbrook, County Armagh; the roadside van bomb is believed to be the largest used by the IRA up to that point.
15.	24th May: The 32nd Cannes Film Festival comes to a close. Apocalypse Now, directed by Francis Ford Coppola, and Die Biechtrommel, directed by Volker Schlondorff, are jointly awarded the Palme d'Or.
16.	June: McDonald's introduces the first U.S. nationwide Happy Meal - it has a circus wagon train theme and costs $1.00.
17.	4th June: Joe Clark is sworn in as the youngest Prime Minister in Canadian history, taking office the day before his 40th birthday. In so doing he defeats the Liberal government of Pierre Trudeau and ends sixteen years of continuous Liberal rule.
18.	1st July: Sony introduces the Walkman TPS-L2, a blue and silver cassette player that runs off two AA batteries. Initially released in Japan, the company predicted only 5,000 would sell but instead its popularity skyrocketed and within the first two months Sony sold more than 50,000 Walkmans costing around $200 each. *Fun Facts: The original idea for a portable stereo is credited to Brazilian-German inventor Andreas Pavel who patented the Stereobelt in 1977. Though Sony agreed to pay Pavel royalties, it refused to recognise him as the inventor of the personal stereo until a legal settlement in 2003. The Walkman sold in excess of 385 million units between 1979 and 2009.*
19.	11th July: NASA's first orbiting space station Skylab starts to disintegrate as it re-enters the atmosphere after being in orbit for 6 years and 2 months.
20.	16th July: President Hasan al-Bakr resigns and is succeeded by Vice President Saddam Hussein in Iraq. *Follow Up: In 2003 a coalition led by the U.S. invaded Iraq to depose Hussein, in which U.S. President George W. Bush and British Prime Minister Tony Blair falsely accused him of possessing weapons of mass destruction and having ties to al-Qaeda. Hussein's Ba'ath party was disbanded and elections were held. Following his capture on the 13th December 2003 his trial took place under the Iraqi Interim Government. On the 5th November 2006, Hussein was convicted by an Iraqi court of crimes against humanity relating to the 1982 killing of 148 Iraqi Shi'a, and he was sentenced to death by hanging. He was executed on the 30th December 2006.*
21.	19th July: Two gigantic supertankers, the Atlantic Empress and the Aegean Captain, collide off the island of Tobago in the Caribbean Sea, killing 26 crew members and spilling 280,000 tons of crude oil into the sea - at the time it was the worst oil-tanker accident in history.

22. | 22nd July: The 66th Tour de France come to a close after 24 stages covering a total distance of 2,339 miles (3,765km). For the second year running the winner was Bernard Hinault of France. *Fun Fact: Hinault won the race a total of five times - 1978, 1979, 1981, 1982 and 1985.*

23. 10th August: Michael Jackson releases his first breakthrough album 'Off the Wall' - the album goes on to sell over 8 million copies in the United States alone. *Fun Facts: Michael Jackson is one of the few artists to have been inducted into the Rock and Roll Hall of Fame twice (he has also been inducted into the Songwriters Hall of Fame and the Dance Hall of Fame). His other achievements include multiple Guinness World Records, 13 Grammy Awards, 24 American Music Awards (more than any other artist), 13 No.1 singles in the U.S. and 7 No.1's in the U.K., and estimated sales of over 350 million records worldwide. His follow up album to Off the Wall, Thriller, is the best-selling album of all time, with sales of over 66 million copies worldwide.*

24. | 21st August: Daniel E. Chadwick receives a patent for his invention of the snowboard.
25. | 1st September: The 571lb (259kg) robotic space probe Pioneer 11 becomes the first spacecraft to visit Saturn - at its closest point it passes the planet at a distance of 13,000 miles.
26. | 27th October: Mother Teresa of Calcutta (b. Anjezë Gonxhe Bojaxhiu, August 26, 1910 - d. September 5, 1997) is awarded Nobel Peace Prize. *Fun Fact: Mother Teresa was declared a saint by Pope Francis in 2016.*
27. | 9th November: NORAD computers at the Alternate National Military Command Center in Fort Ritchie, Maryland, detect a purported massive Soviet nuclear strike. Strategic Air Command are notified and nuclear bombers prepared for takeoff. Within six to seven minutes of the initial response satellite and radar systems are able to confirm that the attack is a false alarm - it was found that a training scenario had been inadvertently loaded into an operational computer.
28. | December: The World Health Organization certifies the global eradication of smallpox. *Historic Facts: The earliest evidence of smallpox dates back to the 3rd century BC in Egyptian mummies. In the 20th century it is estimated that smallpox resulted in 300-500 million deaths - the last naturally occurring case was diagnosed in October 1977.*

29.	1st December: The world's first mobile phone network, Nippon Telegraph and Telephone Corporation (NTT), is launched into commercial operation in Tokyo, Japan. *Fun Fact: The first commercial U.K. phone calls were made on Cellnet and Vodafone (then called Racal-Vodafone and Securicor-Cellnet) on the 1st January 1985.*
30.	3rd December: Ayatollah Ruhollah Khomeini becomes the 1st Supreme Leader of Iran.
31.	3rd December: Eleven fans are killed during a stampede for seats before the rock band the Who perform at Riverfront Coliseum in Cincinnati, Ohio - the concert went on as planned, with the band members not told of the tragedy until after their performance.
32.	15th December: Whilst playing Scrabble and drinking beer Canadians Chris Haney and Scott Abbott decide to create their own game - Trivial Pursuit. *Fun Facts: Trivial Pursuit was released in 1981 and since then has sold more 100 million copies in 26 countries (in 17 languages). Total estimated sales to date are around $2 billion.*

33. 17th December: The three wheeled Budweiser Rocket car driven by Stanley Barrett claims to break the sound barrier by reaching a speed of 739.666mph, or Mach 1.01, during a run on Rogers Dry Lake at Edwards Air Force Base (no independent authority sanctioned the performance). *Fun Fact: The British Thrust SSC became the first officially recognized car to break the sound barrier in 1997 with an average speed of 763.035mph (1227.99km/h) on a measured mile in both directions. The Trust SSC weighed nearly 10 tons and had a total thrust of 223kN.*

34.	24th December: The Ariane 1 rocket makes its maiden flight. Developed and operated by the European Space Agency, Ariane 1 is the first launcher to be developed with the primary purpose of sending commercial satellites into geosynchronous orbit.
35.	24th December: Soviet forces invade Afghanistan to prop up the Communist government, beginning a disastrous and failed ten-year war.

BIRTHS
U.K. PERSONALITIES
BORN IN 1979

William Robert 'Will' Young
20th January 1979

Singer-songwriter and actor who came to prominence after winning the 2002 inaugural series of the ITV talent contest Pop Idol. His double A-sided debut single, Anything Is Possible / Evergreen, was released two weeks after the show's finale and became the fastest-selling debut single in the UK. Young has also acted in film, on stage and in television, and for the 2013 London revival of the musical Cabaret he was nominated for the Laurence Olivier Award for Best Actor.

Rosamund Mary Ellen Pike
27th January 1979

Actress who made her screen debut in the television film A Rather English Marriage (1998), and followed this with roles in the serials Wives And Daughters (1999) and Love In A Cold Climate (2001). Pike received international recognition for her big screen debut as Bond girl Miranda Frost in Die Another Day (2002), and has since starred in films such as The Libertine (2004), Pride & Prejudice (2005), An Education (2009), Jack Reacher (2012) and Gone Girl (2014).

Peter Daniell Doherty
12th March 1979

Musician, songwriter, actor, poet, writer and artist who is best known for being co-frontman of the Libertines, which he formed with Carl Barât in 1997 - his other musical projects include indie band Babyshambles, and Peter Doherty and the Puta Madres. In spite of the Libertines critical and commercial success the band's music was often eclipsed by its internal conflicts stemming primarily from Doherty's addictions to crack cocaine and heroin.

Sophie Michelle Ellis-Bextor
10th April 1979

Singer, songwriter and model who first came to prominence in the late 1990s as the lead singer of the indie rock band Theaudience. After the group disbanded Ellis-Bextor went solo achieving widespread success in the early 2000s. Her solo and most successful album to date was her debut album, Read My Lips, which was released in September 2001. The album reached No.2 in the UK Albums Chart and was certified double platinum by the British Phonographic Industry (BPI).

Luke George Evans
15th April 1979

Actor who began his career on the stage performing in many of London's West End productions such as, Rent, Miss Saigon, and Piaf, before getting his Hollywood breakthrough role starring in Clash Of The Titans (2010). Since then he has had roles in films such as Immortals (2011), The Three Musketeers (2011), The Raven (2012), Fast & Furious 6 (2013), and Peter Jackson's three-part adaptation of The Hobbit. In 2017 Evans starred as Gaston in Disney's Beauty And The Beast.

James McAvoy Jr.
21st April 1979

Actor who made his debut as a teen in The Near Room (1995). His other works include roles in State Of Play (2003), The Last King Of Scotland (2006), Atonement (2007), Filth (2013), and Professor Charles Xavier in the X-Men films. McAvoy has performed in several West End productions and received three nominations for the Laurence Olivier Award for Best Actor. He has also done voice work for animated films including Arthur Christmas (2011) and Gnomeo & Juliet (2011).

Jonathan Peter 'Jonny' Wilkinson, CBE
25th May 1979

Former rugby union player who has represented England and the British and Irish Lions. He rose to prominence before and during the 2003 Rugby World Cup, and is widely acknowledged as one of the best rugby union players of all time. Wilkinson is currently a studio pundit for ITV Sport working on their coverage of the Six Nations Championship and the Rugby World Cup. He was inducted into the World Rugby Hall of Fame on the 17th November 2016.

Richard Abidin Breen
29th June 1979

English-turkish rapper, singer, songwriter, DJ, producer and TV personality better known as Abz Love. Love has sold over 20 million records as a member of, and lead singer of, Simon Cowell's boy band Five. In 2003 he released his debut solo album Abstract Theory which earned him a three top ten hits. After years out of the spotlight Love returned to screens on ITV2's The Big Reunion (2012), and became the runner-up on Channel 5's Celebrity Big Brother 12 (2013).

Allister 'Ali' Carter
25th July 1979

Snooker player who turned professional in 1996 and first gained recognition in 1999 after winning the Benson and Hedges Championship, and the WPBSA Association Young Player of the Year award. Carter is a two-time World Championship runner-up (2008 and 2012), twice losing to Ronnie O'Sullivan. He has also won four ranking titles and been as high as second in the world rankings. His nickname, The Captain, comes from his hobby of piloting aeroplanes.

Lance Sergeant
Johnson Gideon Beharry, VC, COG
26th July 1979

A British Army soldier who, on the 18th March 2005, was awarded the Victoria Cross, the highest military decoration for valour in the British and Commonwealth armed forces. He received the medal for saving members of his unit, the 1st Battalion Princess of Wales's Royal Regiment, from ambushes in May and June 2004 at Al-Amarah, Iraq, sustaining serious head injuries in the latter engagement. As of 2018 he was still a serving member of the armed forces.

David Jonathan Healy, MBE
5th August 1979

A former footballer, and now football manager, who is in charge at NIFL Premiership club Linfield. As a striker he is the all-time leading scorer for Northern Ireland with 36 goals and also shares the record for the highest scoring tally during a UEFA European Championship qualifying campaign with 13 goals. He began his management career with Linfield in October 2015, and led the club to a NIFL Premiership, Irish Cup and County Antrim Shield treble in 2017.

Jamie Cullum
20th August 1979

Singer-songwriter and radio presenter. Although primarily a vocalist and pianist, he also accompanies himself on other instruments including guitar and drums. Cullum's second studio album, Twentysomething, released in October 2003, went platinum and became the No.1 selling studio album by a jazz artist in the United Kingdom (he ended 2003 as the UK's biggest selling jazz artist of all time). Cullum currently presents a weekly evening jazz show on BBC Radio 2.

Wesley Michael Brown
13th October 1979

Professional footballer who began his career with Manchester United after joining the club's academy at the age of 12 in 1992. After turning professional in 1996 he made his senior debut in 1998. Brown became a regular fixture in the first team from 2000 onwards and over the next eight years won numerous honours including four Premier League titles. Brown earned his first England cap in 1999 and was selected to play at the 2002 World Cup.

Aaron William Hughes
8th November 1979

Professional footballer who plays in defence for Scottish Premiership side Heart of Midlothian. He is renowned for his disciplined defending having made 455 Premier League appearances without getting sent off, which is the second-most in the history of the league behind only Ryan Giggs. Hughes made his full international debut aged 18 in 1998 and has earned 110 caps for Northern Ireland, the second most in the nation's history behind goalkeeper Pat Jennings.

Caroline Louise Flack
9th November 1979

Television presenter, radio presenter and model, whose career began when she starred in Bo' Selecta! in 2002, but who has since gone on to present various ITV2 spin-off shows such as I'm A Celebrity... Get Me Out of Here! NOW! (2009-2010) and The Xtra Factor (2011-2013). Flack won the twelfth series of Strictly Come Dancing in 2014 and the following year began presenting series such as Love Island (2015-present) and The X Factor (2015).

Kelly Brook
23rd November 1979

Model, actress and television presenter, who is probably best known for her modelling work in the UK. Her television work has included being a co-presenter on the Big Breakfast (1999), as well as being a team captain on both Celebrity Juice (2013) and It's Not Me, It's You (2016). Brook was crowned FHM's Sexiest Woman In The World in 2005 and as of 2015 had appeared in every FHM 100 Sexiest countdown since 1998.

Simon Marc Amstell
29th November 1979

Comedian, screenwriter, director, television presenter and actor. He best known for his roles as the host of Popworld (2000-2006) and Never Mind the Buzzcocks (2006-2009), being the co-writer and star of the sitcom Grandma's House (2010-2012), and for writing and directing the films Carnage (2017) and Benjamin (2018). Amstell also performs as a stand-up comedian and has performed at the Edinburgh Festival Fringe 4 times (2005, 2006, 2007 and 2009).

Michael James Owen
14th December 1979

Former footballer who played as a striker for Liverpool, Real Madrid, Newcastle United, Manchester United and Stoke City, and became the youngest player to reach 100 goals in the Premier League. Internationally Owen first played for the England senior team in 1998 and eventually went on to score 40 goals in the 89 appearances he made for his country. Since retiring from football he has become a racehorse breeder and owner.

Charlotte Marie 'Lottie' Edwards, CBE
17th December 1979

Former professional cricketer who was captain of the England women's team on 220 occasions - the team won three Ashes series (2008, 2013 and 2014) and the World Cup/World Twenty20 double in 2009 under her captaincy. She is the first player, either male or female, to score 2500 runs in T20 internationals, and in 2014 was appointed a CBE for her services to cricket. Edwards announced her retirement from international cricket in May 2016 and from all cricket in September 2017.

NOTABLE BRITISH DEATHS

16th Jan	Peter William Shorrocks Butterworth (b. 4th February 1919) - Comedy actor and comedian best known for his appearances in the Carry On series of films.
2nd Feb	Sid Vicious (b. Simon John Ritchie; 10th May 1957) - Bass guitarist and vocalist who achieved fame as a member of the punk band the Sex Pistols.
9th Feb	Dennis Gabor (b. 5th June 1900) - Hungarian-British electrical engineer and physicist who received the 1971 Nobel Prize in Physics for inventing holography.
14th Feb	Reginald Maudling (b. 7th March 1917) - Politician who held several Cabinet posts including that of Chancellor of the Exchequer.
19th Mar	Richard Arthur Beckinsale (b. 6th July 1947) - Actor who played Lennie Godber in the BBC sitcom Porridge (along with its sequel series Going Straight) and Alan Moore in the ITV sitcom Rising Damp.
22nd Mar	Sir Richard Adam Sykes, KCMG, MC (b. 8th May 1920) - British Ambassador to the Netherlands.
24th Mar	Sir John Edward 'Jack' Cohen (b. Jacob Edward Kohen; 6th October 1898) - Grocer who founded the Tesco supermarket chain.

IN MEMORY OF
AIREY NEAVE DSO OBE MC
MERTON 1934-8 STEWARD OF THE JCR
MP FOR ABINGDON 1953~79
KILLED OUTSIDE THE HOUSE OF COMMONS
ON 30 MARCH 1979
A MAN OF GREAT COURAGE

30th March - Airey Middleton Sheffield Neave, DSO, OBE, MC, TD (b. 23rd January 1916) - Soldier, lawyer and Member of Parliament. During World War II Neave was the first British prisoner-of-war to succeed in escaping from Oflag IV-C at Colditz Castle, and later worked for MI9. After the war he served with the International Military Tribunal at the Nuremberg Trials and later became a Tory Member of Parliament for Abingdon. He was assassinated in a car bomb attack outside the House of Commons, the Irish National Liberation Army claimed responsibility.

20th Apr	Peter Donald (b. 6th June 1918) - British-born actor who worked in American radio and television. He has been called "one of radio's great dialecticians".
8th Jun	Sir Norman Bishop Hartnell, KCVO (b. 12th June 1901) - Leading British fashion designer best known for his work for the ladies of the Royal Family. Hartnell gained the Royal Warrant as Dressmaker to Queen Elizabeth The Queen Mother in 1940 and Royal Warrant as Dressmaker to Queen Elizabeth II in 1957.

8th Aug	Lieutenant Commander Nicholas John Turney Monsarrat, FRSL, RNVR (b. 22nd March 1910) - Novelist known today for his sea stories, particularly The Cruel Sea (1951) and Three Corvettes (1942-1945), but perhaps best known internationally for his novels, The Tribe That Lost Its Head and its sequel, Richer Than All His Tribe.
27th Aug	Admiral of the Fleet Louis Francis Albert Victor Nicholas Mountbatten, 1st Earl Mountbatten of Burma, KG, GCB, OM, GCSI, GCIE, GCVO, DSO, PC, FRS (b. Prince Louis of Battenberg; 25th June 1900) - Royal Navy officer and statesman who served as the Supreme Allied Commander, South East Asia Command (1943-1946), the last Viceroy of India (1947), the first Governor-General of independent India (1947-1948), First Sea Lord (1954-1959), and thereafter until 1965 as Chief of the Defence Staff.
31st Aug	Ernest James 'Tiger' Smith (b. 6th February 1886) - Cricket player who played in 11 Test Matches between 1911 and 1914. He later became a successful umpire, umpiring several Test matches between 1933 and 1938.
27th Sep	Dame Gracie Fields, DBE (b. Grace Stansfield; 9th January 1898) - Actress, singer, comedienne and star of both cinema and music hall.
27th Sep	James McCulloch (b. 4th June 1953) - Musician and songwriter best known for playing lead and bass guitar as a member of Paul McCartney's band Wings (1974-1977).
13th Oct	Rebecca Clarke (b. 27th August 1886) - Classical composer and violist best known for her chamber music featuring the viola.

30th October 1979 - Sir Barnes Neville Wallis, CBE, FRS, RDI, FRAeS (b. 26th September 1887) - Scientist, engineer and inventor who is best known for inventing the bouncing bomb used by the Royal Air Force in Operation Chastise (the Dambusters raid) to attack the dams of the Ruhr Valley during World War II. Among his other inventions were his version of the geodetic airframe and the earthquake bomb.

23rd Nov	Merle Oberon (b. Estelle Merle O'Brien Thompson; 19th February 1911) - Anglo-Indian actress who was nominated for an Academy Award for Best Actress for her role as Kitty Vane in The Dark Angel (1935).
30th Nov	Joyce Irene Grenfell, OBE (b. 10th February 1910) - Comedienne, singer, actress and soliloquist.
9th Dec	Israel Jacob 'Jack' Solomons, OBE (b. 8th December 1902) - Boxing promoter who has been referred to as one of the greatest boxing promoters in history and England's greatest boxing impresario.

1979 TOP 10 SINGLES

No.1	Bright Eyes - *Art Garfunkel*
No.2	We Don't Talk Anymore - *Cliff Richard*
No.3	When You're In Love With A Beautiful Woman - *Dr Hook*
No.4	Are 'Friends' Electric? - *Tubeway Army*
No.5	I Will Survive - *Gloria Gaynor*
No.6	I Don't Like Mondays - *Boomtown Rats*
No.7	Heart Of Glass - *Blondie*
No.8	One Day At A Time - *Lena Martell*
No.9	Sunday Girl - *Blondie*
No.10	Dance Away - *Roxy Music*

1 Art Garfunkel
Bright Eyes

Label:	Written by:	Length:
CBS	Mike Batt	4 mins

Arthur Ira Garfunkel (b. 5th November 1941) is a singer, poet, math teacher and actor who is best known for his partnership with Paul Simon in the folk-rock duo Simon & Garfunkel. Through his solo and collaborative work Garfunkel has earned eight Grammys, including a Lifetime Achievement Award, and in 1990 he and Simon were inducted into the Rock and Roll Hall of Fame. 'Bright Eyes' was used in the soundtrack of the 1978 animated adventure/drama film Watership Down, and was the biggest-selling single of 1979 in the UK - it remained at No.1 for six weeks and sold over a million copies.

---

2 Cliff Richard
We Don't Talk Anymore

Label:	Written by:	Length:
EMI	Alan Tarney	4 mins 11 secs

Sir Cliff Richard, OBE (b. Harry Rodger Webb; 14th October 1940) is a pop singer, musician, performer, actor and philanthropist who has total sales of over 21 million singles in the UK and over 250 million records worldwide. He is the third-top-selling artist in UK Singles Chart history behind only the Beatles and Elvis Presley. 'We Don't Talk Anymore' reached the No.1 spot in August 1979 and became Richard's tenth UK No.1 record (his first since Congratulations in 1968).

Dr Hook
When You're In Love With A Beautiful Woman

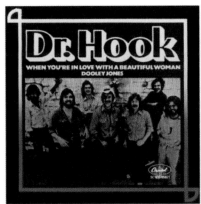

Label:	Written by:	Length:
Capitol Records	Even Stevens	2 mins 58 secs

Dr. Hook, formerly Dr Hook & the Medicine Show, was an American rock band formed in New Jersey, United States, who had eight years of regular chart hits in both the U.S. and the UK. 'When You're in Love with a Beautiful Woman' first appeared on the band's 1978 album Pleasure and Pain and became an international hit. It reached No.6 on the Billboard Hot 100 singles chart in the USA, and did even better in the UK where it spent three weeks at No.1 in November 1979.

Tubeway Army
Are 'Friends' Electric?

Label:	Written by:	Length:
Beggars Banquet	Gary Numan	5 mins 48 secs

Tubeway Army were a new wave and electronic band led by lead singer Gary Numan (b. 8th March 1958). They were the first band of the electronic era to have a synthesiser-based No.1 hit, with their single 'Are 'Friends' Electric?' and its parent album Replicas both topping the UK charts in mid-1979. After its release Numan opted to drop the Tubeway Army name and release music under his own name as he was the sole songwriter, producer and public face of the band, but he retained the musicians from Tubeway Army as his backing band.

Gloria Gaynor
I Will Survive

Label:	**Written by:**	**Length:**
Polydor	Fekaris / Perren	3 mins 15 secs

Gloria Gaynor (b. Gloria Fowles; 7th September 1949) is an American singer best known for the disco era hits 'I Will Survive' (her only UK No.1 single) and 'Never Can Say Goodbye' (1974). 'I Will Survive' was originally released as the B-side to a cover version of the Righteous Brothers song 'Substitute' but became a worldwide hit for Gaynor when disc jockeys decided to play it instead of the A-side. It went on to sell over 14 million copies worldwide and has remained a popular disco anthem ever since.

Boomtown Rats
I Don't Like Mondays

Label:	**Written by:**	**Length:**
Ensign	Bob Geldof	3 mins 47 secs

The **Boomtown Rats** are an Irish rock band that is led by vocalist Bob Geldof. The original line-up consisted of Garry Roberts (lead guitar), Johnnie Fingers (keyboard), Pete Briquette (bass), Gerry Cott (rhythm guitar) and Simon Crowe (drums). 'I Don't Like Mondays' was written about the 1979 Cleveland Elementary School shooting in San Diego, United States, and went to No.1 for four weeks during the summer of 1979.

7 Blondie
Heart Of Glass

Label:	Written by:	Length:
Chrysalis	Stein / Harry	3 mins 54 secs

Blondie is an American rock band founded by singer Debbie Harry (b. Angela Trimble; 1st July 1945) and guitarist Chris Stein (b. 5th January 1950), and was a pioneer in the early new wave and punk scenes of the mid-late 1970s. 'Heart of Glass' featured on the band's third studio album, Parallel Lines (1978), and was released as the album's third single in January 1979. It reached No.1 one on the charts in several countries, including the United States and the United Kingdom, and helped propel Blondie from cult group to mainstream icons.

8 Lena Martell
One Day At A Time

Label:	Written by:	Length:
Pye Records	Wilkin / Kristofferson	3 mins 12 secs

Lena Martell (b. Helen Thomson; 15th May 1940) is a Scottish singer who had a No.1 UK single with 'One Day at a Time' in October 1979. Her follow-up singles failed to chart so she has the dubious honour of being classified as a one-hit wonder despite her success in the Albums Chart (she placed six albums in the UK Albums Chart between 1974 and 1980, including four that reached the Top 20). 'One Day at a Time' is a popular Country and Western-style Christian song that was written by Marijohn Wilkin and Kris Kristofferson; it has been recorded by over 200 artists and has reached No.1 in several territories.

Blondie
Sunday Girl

Label:	Written by:	Length:
Chrysalis	Chris Stein	3 mins 1 sec

Sunday Girl was written and recorded by Blondie in 1978 and was the fourth single to be taken from the album Parallel Lines. The track was a No.1 hit in the UK Singles Chart for three weeks in May 1979, but despite this was not released as a single in the United States. Blondie have since had a further four No.1 records in the United Kingdom, and in total have sold more than 40 million records worldwide. In 2006 the original group members were inducted into the Rock and Roll Hall of Fame.

Roxy Music
Dance Away

Label:	Written by:	Length:
Polydor	Bryan Ferry	3 mins 45 secs

Roxy Music were a rock band formed in 1970 by Bryan Ferry, who became the band's lead vocalist and chief songwriter, and bassist Graham Simpson. Alongside Ferry the other members of the group in 1979 were Phil Manzanera, Andy Mackay, Gary Tibbs, Paul Thompson, Dave Skinner and Paul Carrack. 'Dance Away' was the second single to be taken from the album Manifesto and became one of the band's most famous songs; it reached No.2 in the UK and spent a total of 14 weeks on the charts, the longest chart residency of any Roxy Music single. Their only No.1 record in the UK came in February 1981 when 'Jealous Guy' topped the charts.

1979: TOP FILMS

1. **Kramer vs. Kramer** - *Columbia*
2. **The Amityville Horror** - *American International Pictures*
3. **Rocky II** - *United Artists*
4. **Apocalypse Now** - *United Artists*
5. **Star Trek: The Motion Picture** - *Paramount*

OSCARS

Best Picture: Kramer vs. Kramer

Most Nominations: All That Jazz and Kramer vs. Kramer (9)

Most Wins: Kramer vs. Kramer (5)

Best Director: Robert Benton - *Kramer vs. Kramer*

Best Actor: Dustin Hoffman - *Kramer vs. Kramer*
Best Actress: Sally Field - *Norma Rae*
Best Supporting Actor: Melvyn Douglas - *Being There*
Best Supporting Actress: Meryl Streep - *Kramer vs. Kramer*

The 52nd Academy Awards were presented on the 14th April 1980.

Columbia Pictures Presents A Stanley Jaffe Production

Dustin Hoffman
in
Kramer vs. Kramer

Meryl Streep   Jane Alexander

Directed by: Robert Benton - Runtime: 1 hour 45 minutes

Ted Kramer's wife Joanna leaves him allowing for a lost bond to be rediscovered between Ted and his son Billy. A heated battle then ensues over Billy as Ted and Joanna go to court to fight for custody of their son.

STARRING

Dustin Hoffman
Born: 8ᵗʰ August 1937

Character:
Ted Kramer

Actor and director with a career in film, television and theatre since 1960. His breakthrough film role came in 1967 when he played the title character Benjamin Braddock in the The Graduate. Hoffman has been nominated for seven Academy Awards, winning twice for Best Actor in Kramer vs. Kramer (1979) and Rain Man (1988). He has also won six Golden Globes (including an honorary one) and four BAFTAs.

Meryl Streep
Born: 22ⁿᵈ June 1949

Character:
Joanna Kramer

Actress born Mary Louise Streep who is often described as the 'best actress of her generation'. Nominated for a record 21 Academy Awards, she has won three. Streep has received 31 Golden Globe nominations, winning eight - more nominations and wins than any other actor. She has also won three Primetime Emmy Awards and has been nominated for fifteen British Academy Film Awards, and seventeen Screen Actors Guild Awards, winning two of each.

Jane Alexander
Born: 28ᵗʰ October 1939

Character:
Margaret Phelps

Author, actress, and former director of the National Endowment for the Arts. Alexander made her Broadway debut in 1968 in The Great White Hope and won the 1969 Tony Award for Best Featured Actress in a Play. In total she has received seven Tony Award nominations and was inducted into the American Theater Hall of Fame in 1994. In film she has received four Academy Award nominations for her performances; Kramer vs. Kramer earned her her third nomination.

TRIVIA

Goofs	Ted Kramer's lawyer tells him that if he wishes to appeal the decision granting custody to his ex-wife his son would have to take the stand. On an appeal no new evidence is called upon and therefore the son would not be called as a witness.
	The trees are green in the scenes which supposedly take place in New York at Halloween and Christmas.
Interesting Facts	Meryl Streep wrote her own courtroom speech upon writer and director Robert Benton's suggestion after she told him she wasn't satisfied with the way it was originally written.

CONTINUED

Interesting Facts The strength of the performances of the two leads can be at least partly attributed to what was going on in their private lives at the time. Hoffman was in the midst of a messy divorce while Streep was still recovering from the death of her lover John Cazale.

Dustin Hoffman planned the moment when he throws his wine glass against the wall during the restaurant scene with Meryl Streep. The only person he warned in advance was the cameraman, to make sure that it got in the shot. Streep's shocked reaction was real, but she stayed in character long enough for writer and director Robert Benton to yell cut. In the documentary on the DVD she recalls yelling at Hoffman as soon as the shot was over for scaring her so badly.

Meryl Streep left her just-claimed Oscar for the film on the back of a toilet during the 1980 festivities.

When Justin Henry, who played the Kramer's son Billy, was nominated for the Academy Award for Best Actor in a Supporting Role, Henry, at the age of eight, became the youngest person to be nominated for this award, as well as the youngest Oscar nominee in any category, a record which still stands today.

Quote **Billy Kramer**: When's Mommy coming back?
Ted Kramer: I dont know, Billy. Soon.
Billy Kramer: How soon?
Ted Kramer: Soon.
Billy Kramer: Will she pick me up after school?
Ted Kramer: Probably. And if she doesn't I will.
Billy Kramer: What if you forget?
Ted Kramer: I won't forget.
Billy Kramer: What if you get run over by a truck and get killed?
Ted Kramer: Then Mommy will pick you up.

THE AMITYVILLE HORROR

Directed by: Stuart Rosenberg - Runtime: 1 hour 57 minutes

Newlyweds move into a large house where a mass murder was committed and experience strange manifestations which drive them away.

STARRING

James Brolin
Born: 18th July 1940

Character:
George Lutz

Actor, producer and director born Craig Kenneth Bruderlin. He is best known for his roles in film and television, including sitcoms and soap operas - he is currently playing the role of John, the family patriarch, in the CBS comedy Life in Pieces. He is the father of actor Josh Brolin and husband of Barbra Streisand. Brolin has won two Golden Globes and an Emmy, and received a star on the Hollywood Walk of Fame on the 10th August 2016.

Margot Kidder
Born: 17th October 1948
Died: 13th May 2018

Character:
Kathy Lutz

A Canadian-American actress and activist whose career spanned over five decades. She started out in the 1960s appearing in low-budget Canadian films and television series before landing a lead role in Quackser Fortune Has a Cousin in the Bronx (1970). Her accolades include three Canadian Screen Awards and one Daytime Emmy Award. Kidder is most widely known for her performances as Lois Lane in the Superman film series.

Rod Steiger
Born: 14th April 1925
Died: 9th July 2002

Character:
Father Delaney

Actor noted for his portrayal of offbeat, often volatile and crazed characters. He made his film debut in Teresa (1951), and subsequently appeared in films such as Oklahoma! (1955), Across the Bridge (1957) and Al Capone (1959). Other notable roles include starring as Marlon Brando's mobster brother Charley in On the Waterfront (1954), Sol Nazerman in The Pawnbroker (1964), and Bill Gillespie (opposite Sidney Poitier) in In the Heat of the Night (1967), which won him the Academy Award for Best Actor.

TRIVIA

Goofs | When the cheek-pinching Aunt Helena arrives (at around 36 mins), Matthew answers the door with a very red left cheek from a previous take.

Toward the end of the film lightning smashes through one of the attic windows (during the axe attack), but subsequent exterior shots (the escape) show both windows still intact.

Interesting Facts | At the time of its release the film was one of the highest grossing independent films of all time, and was American International Pictures' biggest hit.

CONTINUED

Interesting Facts

James Brolin was hesitant when he was first offered the role of George Lutz. He was told that there was no script and that he must obtain a copy of Jay Anson's novel and read it as soon as possible. Brolin started the book one evening at seven o'clock and was still reading at two o'clock in the morning. He had hung a pair of his trousers up in the room earlier and at a really tense part in the book the trousers fell down unexpectedly, causing Brolin to jump out of his chair and nearly hit his head on the ceiling. It was then that Brolin thought, "there's something to this story" and agreed to do the film.

While shooting the scene where Kathy Lutz is startled by the red eyes in the window, director Stuart Rosenberg wasn't impressed by Margot Kidder's reaction. According to Kidder, Rosenberg then tried to hold up a "a day-glo orange stuffed velour pig with glass eyes" in an attempt to startle her. The result, far from frightening her, was merely hysterical laughter.

As the film was made on a relatively modest budget James Brolin took less money up front and agreed to take 10% of the gross sales after its release. After the film became an unexpected blockbuster (at that time it was in the top ten of all time), he eventually received about $17 million - if adjusted for inflation that would be equivalent to a little over $59 million as of 2018.

In hopes of creating more publicity for the film the studio concocted stories of "weird" occurrences on the set of the film.

Due to all the unwanted fame the book and film had brought upon the real house in Amityville, the current owners have replaced the "evil eyes" windows with normal rectangle-shaped windows.

Quotes

Kathy Lutz: I just wish that... all those people hadn't died here. I mean... ugh! A guy kills his whole family. Doesn't that bother you?
George Lutz: Well, sure, but... houses don't have memories.

The House: GET OUT!

Directed by: Sylvester Stallone - Runtime: 1 hour 59 minutes

Rocky runs into financial and family problems after his bout with Apollo Creed. The embarrassed champ meanwhile goads him into getting back in the ring for a rematch.

STARRING

Sylvester Stallone
Born: 6th July 1946

Character:
Rocky Balboa

Actor, screenwriter, producer and director. Stallone is well known for his Hollywood action roles, in particular as boxer Rocky Balboa in the Rocky series of seven films (1976-2015), but also as soldier John Rambo from the four Rambo films (1982-2008) and Barney Ross in the three The Expendables movies (2010-2014). Stallone wrote or co-wrote most of the 14 films in all three franchises and also directed many of them.

Talia Shire
Born: 25th April 1946

Characters:
Adrian

Actress who first became famous for her role of Connie Corleone in The Godfather and its sequels, for which she was nominated for the Academy Award for Best Supporting Actress in The Godfather: Part II. In Rocky she portrayed Adrian Pennino Balboa and was nominated for a second Academy Award for Best Actress. She has also starred in films such as Kiss the Bride (2002), I ♥ Huckabees (2004) and Homo Erectus (2007).

Burt Young
Born: 30th April 1940

Character:
Paulie

Actor, painter and author born Gerald Tommaso DeLouise. He is best known for his Academy Award-nominated role as Sylvester Stallone's brother-in-law and best friend Paulie Pennino in the Rocky film series. As a painter Young's art has been displayed in galleries throughout the world and as a published author his works include two filmed screenplays and a 400-page historically based novel called Endings.

TRIVIA

Goofs	It's well established that Rocky is left handed, however when he signs an autograph for the nurse at the beginning of the movie he uses his right hand.
	When Adrian is in a coma, Rocky's facial hair is used to give a general idea of time. Just before Adrian comes out of the coma you can see Rocky with almost a full beard. The shot pans over to Adrian opening her eyes. When the shot pans back to Rocky he barely has a 5 o'clock shadow.
Interesting Facts	When Rocky is training for the fight he is sparring with a smaller quicker fighter, the sparring partner is played by real life Champion Roberto Durán.

Interesting Facts | Analysis by Philadelphia locals tracked the route Rocky took through the city during his training run (when all the children joined him). If he took this actual route from his South Philly house to the top of the Art Museum steps, he would have covered approximately 30 miles!

During his preparation for the film Sylvester Stallone was bench-pressing 220 pounds when the weight fell and tore his right pectoral muscle. This was shortly before the final fight scene was to be filmed and ultimately led to the scene being shot with Stallone still badly injured.

Originally Adrian was supposed to be at the big fight, however, because Talia Shire was working on another movie at the time the storyline was changed to having her stay home and watch the fight on television. The scenes of her watching the boxing match on television were shot and then edited into the movie several months after filming had finished.

It took Sylvester Stallone and editors Danford B. Greene and Stanford C. Allen over eight months to edit the climatic fight scene so as to meet Stallone's approval.

Stallone began working on the Rocky III (1982) script immediately after completing Rocky II, with the intention of the series being a trilogy - he had no intention of making any further Rocky films.

Quotes | *[Mickey has Rocky chase after a chicken as part of his training]*
Rocky Balboa: I feel like a Kentucky Fried idiot.

Rocky Balboa: *[After round 1 of the rematch with Creed]* I can't believe it!
Mickey: What?
Rocky Balboa: He broke my nose again.

Rocky Balboa: I just got one thing to say... to my wife at home: Yo, Adrian! I DID IT!

APOCALYPSE NOW

Directed by: Francis Ford Coppola - Runtime: 2 hours 27 minutes

During the Vietnam War, Captain Willard is sent on a dangerous mission into Cambodia to assassinate a renegade Colonel who has set himself up as a god among a local tribe.

STARRING

Marlon Brando
Born: 3rd April 1924
Died: 1st July 2004

Character:
Colonel Walter E. Kurtz

Actor, film director and activist. He is credited with bringing a gripping realism to film acting and is often cited as one of the greatest and most influential actors of all time. He helped to popularise the Stanislavski system of acting, today more commonly referred to as method acting. Brando is most famous for his Academy Award-winning performances as Terry Malloy in On the Waterfront (1954) and Vito Corleone in The Godfather (1972).

Martin Sheen
Born: 3rd August 1940

Character:
Captain Benjamin L. Willard

American-Irish actor, born Ramón Gerard Antonio Estévez, who first became known for his roles in the films The Subject Was Roses (1968) and Badlands (1973). He later achieved wide recognition for his leading role in Apocalypse Now (1979) and as President Josiah Bartlet in the television series The West Wing (1999-2006). Sheen received a star on the Hollywood Walk of Fame in 1989 and is the father of four children, all of whom are actors.

Robert Duvall
Born: 5th January 1931

Character:
Lieutenant Colonel Bill Kilgore

Actor and filmmaker whose career spans more than six decades. Duvall began appearing in theatre during the late 1950s, moving into television and film roles during the early 1960s. He has been nominated for seven Academy Awards, winning once for his performance in Tender Mercies (1983), seven Golden Globe Awards (winning four), and has multiple nominations and one win each of the BAFTA, Screen Actors Guild Award, and Emmy Award.

TRIVIA

Goofs	During Willard's briefing in Nha Trang, every time someone mentions the name "Kurtz" on the soundtrack, on screen they are mouthing "Lieghley", the original name of Col. Kurtz's character in the script during the early part of the shooting.
	After the canopy of the boat is destroyed and is replaced by giant leaves, it reappears again when they are at the bridge. In subsequent shots it is again replaced by leaves.
Interesting Facts	Laurence Fishburne, who plays Tyrone 'Clean' Miller, was 14 when production began in 1976. He lied about his age.

CONTINUED

Interesting Facts There are no opening credits or titles. The title appears late in the film as graffiti which reads "Our motto: Apocalypse Now". The film could not be copyrighted as "Apocalypse Now" unless the title was seen in the film.

Francis Ford Coppola shot nearly 200 hours of footage during the making of this film.

Most of the dialogue was added in post-production. Extraneous noise such as helicopters left many scenes with unusable audio.

It took Francis Ford Coppola nearly three years to edit the footage. While working on his final edit it became apparent to him that Martin Sheen would be needed to tape several additional narrative voice-overs. Coppola soon discovered that Sheen was busy and unable to perform these voice-overs. He then called in Sheen's brother, Joe Estevez, whose voice sounded nearly identical, to perform the new narrative tracks. Estevez was also used as a stand-in when Sheen suffered a heart attack during the shoot in 1976. Estevez was not credited for his work as a stand-in, nor for his voice-over work.

Robert Duvall's iconic Oscar-nominated performance as Colonel Kilgore amounts to just eleven minutes of screentime.

Quotes *[While flying in a helicopter with Air Cavalry soldiers]*
Chef: Why do all you guys sit on your helmets?
Door Gunner: So we don't get our balls blown off.

Kilgore: I love the smell of napalm in the morning.

STAR TREK: THE MOTION PICTURE

Directed by: Robert Wise - Runtime: 2 hours 12 minutes

When an alien spacecraft of enormous power is spotted approaching Earth, Admiral James T. Kirk resumes command of the overhauled USS Enterprise in order to intercept it.

STARRING

William Shatner
Born: 22nd March 1931

Character:
Captain James T. Kirk

Canadian actor, author, producer, director and singer. In his seven decades of television Shatner has become a cultural icon for his portrayal of James T. Kirk, captain of the USS Enterprise, in the Star Trek franchise. Other notable television appearances include playing the eponymous veteran police sergeant in T.J. Hooker (1982-1986) and hosting Rescue 911 (1989-1996), which won a People's Choice Award for the Favourite New TV Dramatic Series.

Leonard Nimoy
Born: 26th March 1931
Died: 27th February 2015

Character:
Commander Spock

Actor, film director, photographer, author, singer and songwriter. Nimoy began his career in his early twenties teaching acting classes in Hollywood, and making minor film and television appearances throughout the 1950s. He was best known though for his role as Spock of the Star Trek franchise, a character he portrayed in television and film from a pilot episode shot in late 1964 to his final film performance in 2013.

DeForest Kelley
Born: 20th January 1920
Died: 11th June 1999

Character:
Dr. McCoy

Actor, screenwriter, poet and singer. During World War II, Kelley served as an enlisted man in the U.S. Army Air Forces assigned to the First Motion Picture Unit. His acting career began with the feature film Fear in the Night (1947), a low-budget movie that brought him to the attention of a national audience. He was best known for his roles in Westerns and as Dr. Leonard 'Bones' McCoy of the USS Enterprise in the television and film series Star Trek.

TRIVIA

Goofs | In the Original Star Trek Series Spock says that the planet Vulcan has no Moon, but while he is meditating on Vulcan in this film, a Moon can be seen. This anomaly has been fixed in the 'Director's Edition' of the movie with the Moon being removed, and the addition of an actual atmosphere and sky on Vulcan.

William Shatner's hairstyle appears to change in nearly every scene.

Interesting Facts | The cast hated the uniforms which required assistance in order to be removed. In fact one of the cast's conditions for returning in a sequel was that they have new uniforms.

CONTINUED

Interesting Facts
The Klingon words spoken by the Klingon captain were actually invented by James Doohan (Commander Scott). Linguist Marc Okrand later devised grammar and syntax rules for the language, along with more vocabulary words in Star Trek III: The Search for Spock (1984), and wrote a Klingon dictionary. He based all his work on those few Klingon lines in this movie so that they made sense retrospectively.

Persis Khambatta became very emotional about having her head shaved for her role as Lieutenant Ilia. She kept her shorn hair in a box for a time and asked Gene Roddenberry to take out insurance in case her hair did not grow back. It did.

Uhura's communications earpieces are the only props from the original Star Trek (1966) series. They were dug out of storage when it was realised someone had forgotten to make new ones for the movie.

The producers and the cast were very worried about their appearances after being away from Star Trek for ten years. Special lighting and camera tricks were used to hide the cast's aging, and William Shatner went on a near-starvation diet prior to filming. However, in all subsequent Star Trek movies it was decided to make the aging of the crew part of the story.

Quotes
Dr. McCoy: Spock, you haven't changed a bit. You're just as warm and sociable as ever.
Commander Spock: Nor have you, doctor, as your continued predilection for irrelevancy demonstrates.

Captain Kirk: Well, for a man who swore he'd never return to the Starfleet...
Dr. McCoy: Just a moment, Captain, sir. I'll explain what happened. Your revered Admiral Nogura invoked a little-known, seldom-used 'reserve activation clause'. In simpler language, Captain, they DRAFTED me!
Captain Kirk: *[in mock horror]* They didn't.
Dr. McCoy: This was your idea. This was your idea, wasn't it?

SPORTING WINNERS

BBC SPORTS PERSONALITY OF THE YEAR

SEBASTIAN COE - ATHLETICS

Sebastian Newbold Coe, Baron Coe, CH, KBE (b. 29th September 1956), is a politician and former track and field athlete. During his athletics career Coe won four Olympic medals and set eleven world records in middle-distance track events, eight outdoor and three indoor - this included, in 1979, setting three world records in the space of 41 days.

1979	BBC Sports Personality	Country	Sport
Winner	**Sebastian Coe**	**England**	**Athletics**
Runner Up	Ian Botham	England	Cricket
Third Place	Kevin Keegan	England	Football

Major Championship Medals:

Year	Competition	Location	Event	Medal
1978	European Championships	Prague	800m	Bronze
1980	Olympic Games	Moscow	800m	Silver
1980	Olympic Games	Moscow	1500m	Gold
1982	European Championships	Athens	800m	Silver
1984	Olympic Games	Los Angeles	800m	Silver
1984	Olympic Games	Los Angeles	1500m	Gold
1986	European Championships	Stuttgart	800m	Gold
1986	European Championships	Stuttgart	1500m	Silver

FIVE NATIONS RUGBY
WINNERS - WALES

Position	Nation	Played	Won	Draw	Lost	For	Against	+/-	Points
1st	**Wales**	**4**	**3**	**0**	**1**	**83**	**51**	**+32**	**6**
2nd	France	4	2	1	1	50	46	+4	5
3rd	Ireland	4	1	2	1	53	51	+2	4
4th	England	4	1	1	2	24	52	-28	3
5th	Scotland	4	0	2	2	48	58	-10	2

The 1979 Five Nations Championship was the fiftieth series of the rugby union Five Nations Championship. Including the previous incarnations as the Home Nations and Five Nations, this was the eighty-fifth series of the northern hemisphere rugby union championship. Ten matches were played between the 20th January and 17th March, with Wales taking its 21st Championship title and 16th Triple Crown.

Date	Team		Score		Team	Location
20-01-1979	Ireland		9-9		France	Lansdowne Road, Dublin
20-01-1979	Scotland		13-19		Wales	Murrayfield, Edinburgh
03-02-1979	Wales		24-21		Ireland	National Stadium, Cardiff
03-02-1979	England		7-7		Scotland	Twickenham, London
17-02-1979	France		14-13		Wales	Parc des Princes, Paris
17-02-1979	Ireland		12-7		England	Lansdowne Road, Dublin
03-03-1979	England		7-6		France	Twickenham, London
03-03-1979	Scotland		11-11		Ireland	Murrayfield, Edinburgh
17-03-1979	France		21-17		Scotland	Parc des Princes, Paris
17-03-1979	Wales		27-3		England	National Stadium, Cardiff

CALCUTTA CUP

The Calcutta Cup was first awarded in 1879 and is the rugby union trophy awarded to the winner of the match (currently played as part of the Six Nations Championship) between England and Scotland. The Cup was presented to the Rugby Football Union after the Calcutta Football Club in India disbanded in 1878 - it is made from melted down silver rupees withdrawn from the clubs funds.

Historical Records	England	Scotland	Draws
	70 Wins	40 Wins	15

BRITISH GRAND PRIX - CLAY REGAZZONI

Clay Regazzoni at the British Grand Prix at Silverstone.

The 1979 British Grand Prix was held at the Silverstone Circuit on the 14th July. It was round 9 of 15 of both the World Championship of F1 Drivers and the International Cup for F1 Constructors. The 68-lap race was won by Clay Regazzoni, driving a Williams-Ford, and was the first ever Formula One victory for the Williams team.

Pos.	Country	Driver	Constructor
1st	**Switzerland**	**Clay Regazzoni**	**Williams-Ford**
2nd	France	René Arnoux	Renault
3rd	France	Jean-Pierre Jarier	Tyrrell-Ford

1979 GRAND PRIX SEASON

Rnd	Date	Race	Winning Driver	Constructor
1	21st Jan	Argentine Grand Prix	Jacques Laffite	Ligier-Ford
2	4th Feb	Brazilian Grand Prix	Jacques Laffite	Ligier-Ford
3	3rd Mar	South African Grand Prix	Gilles Villeneuve	Ferrari
4	8th Apr	U.S. Grand Prix West	Gilles Villeneuve	Ferrari
5	29th Apr	Spanish Grand Prix	Patrick Depailler	Ligier-Ford
6	13th May	Belgian Grand Prix	Jody Scheckter	Ferrari
7	27th May	Monaco Grand Prix	Jody Scheckter	Ferrari
8	1st Jul	French Grand Prix	Jean-Pierre Jabouille	Renault
9	14th Jul	British Grand Prix	Clay Regazzoni	Williams-Ford
10	29th Jul	German Grand Prix	Alan Jones	Williams-Ford
11	12th Aug	Austrian Grand Prix	Alan Jones	Williams-Ford
12	26th Aug	Dutch Grand Prix	Alan Jones	Williams-Ford
13	9th Sep	Italian Grand Prix	Jody Scheckter	Ferrari
14	30th Sep	Canadian Grand Prix	Alan Jones	Williams-Ford
15	7th oct	U.S. Grand Prix	Gilles Villeneuve	Ferrari

The 1979 Formula One season was the 33rd season of FIA Formula One motor racing and concluded with Jody Scheckter taking the Drivers' Championship title with 51 points. Second and third places went to Gilles Villeneuve and Alan Jones with 47 and 40 points respectively.

GRAND NATIONAL - RUBSTIC

The 1979 Grand National was the 133rd renewal of this world famous horse race and took place at Aintree Racecourse near Liverpool on the 31st March. The race was won by the smallest horse in the field Rubstic who became the first ever Scottish-trained winner.

Thirty-four horses contested the 1979 Grand National; 7 horses completed the course, 12 fell, 7 were brought down, 4 pulled up, 3 unseated their riders and 1 refused. The 6/1 favourite Alverton fell at the 22nd fence and had to be euthanised.

Pos.	Name	Jockey	Age	Weight	Odds
1st	**Rubstic**	**Maurice Barnes**	**10**	**10st-0lb**	**25/1**
2nd	Zongalero	Bob Davies	9	10st-5lb	20/1
3rd	Rough and Tumble	John Francome	9	10st-7lb	14/1
4th	The Pilgarlic	Richard Evans	11	10st-1lb	16/1
5th	Wagner	Ridley Lamb	9	10st-0lb	50/1

GOLF OPEN CHAMPIONSHIP - SEVE BALLESTEROS

Seve Ballesteros wins the 1979 Open and the Claret Jug.

The 1979 Open Championship was the 108th to be played and was held between the 18th and 21st of July at the Royal Lytham & St Annes Golf Club in Lancashire. Seve Ballesteros, 22, won the first of his five major titles, three strokes ahead of runners-up Jack Nicklaus and Ben Crenshaw. It was the first of his three Open Championship victories; he raised the Claret Jug again in 1984 and 1988. In total 152 players took part in the competition which had a total prize fund of £155,000 (Ballesteros' share was £15,000).

FOOTBALL LEAGUE CHAMPIONS

England:

Pos.	Team	P	W	D	L	F	A	Pts.
1st	**Liverpool**		**30**	**8**	**4**	**85**	**16**	**68**
2nd	Nottingham Forest		21	18	3	61	26	60
3rd	West Bromwich Albion		24	11	7	72	35	59
4th	Everton		17	17	8	52	40	51
5th	Leeds United		18	14	10	70	52	50

Scotland:

Pos.	Team	P	W	D	L	F	A	Pts.
1st	**Celtic**	**36**	**21**	**6**	**9**	**61**	**37**	**48**
2nd	Rangers	36	18	9	9	52	35	45
3rd	Dundee United	36	18	8	10	56	37	44
4th	Aberdeen	36	13	14	9	59	36	40
5th	Hibernian	36	12	13	11	44	48	37

FA CUP WINNERS - ARSENAL

Arsenal	3-2	**Manchester United**
Talbot ⚽ 12'		McQueen ⚽ 86'
Stapleton ⚽ 43'		McIlroy ⚽ 88'
Sunderland ⚽ 89'		

Referee: Ron Challis (Kent)

The 1979 FA Cup Final took place on the 12th May at Wembley Stadium in front of 99,219 fans. The match was contested by Arsenal and Manchester United, and with three goals scored in the dying minutes it is regarded as one of the greatest-ever finishes to an FA Cup final (it is often referred to as the 'Five-minute Final').

WIMBLEDON

Björn Borg and Martina Navratilova playing for their 1979 Wimbledon Championship titles.

Men's Singles Champion - Björn Borg - Sweden
Ladies Singles Champion - Martina Navratilova - United States

The 1979 Wimbledon Championships took place on the outdoor grass courts at the All England Lawn Tennis and Croquet Club in Wimbledon, London, and ran from the 25th June until the 7th July. It was the 93rd staging of the Wimbledon Championships and the second Grand Slam tennis event of 1979.

Men's Singles Final:

Country	Player	Set 1	Set 2	Set 3	Set 4	Set 5
Sweden	Björn Borg	6	6	3	6	6
United States	Roscoe Tanner	7	1	6	3	4

Women's Singles Final:

Country	Player	Set 1	Set 2
United States	Martina Navratilova	6	6
United States	Chris Evert Lloyd	4	4

Men's Doubles Final:

Country	Players	Set 1	Set 2	Set 3	Set 4
United States	Peter Fleming / John McEnroe	4	6	6	6
United States / Mexico	Brian Gottfried / Raúl Ramírez	6	4	2	2

Women's Doubles Final:

Country	Players	Set 1	Set 2	Set 3
United States	Billie Jean King / Martina Navratilova	5	6	6
Netherlands / Australia	Betty Stöve / Wendy Turnbull	7	3	2

Mixed Doubles Final:

Country	Players	Set 1	Set 2
South Africa	Bob Hewitt / Greer Stevens	7	7
South Africa / Netherlands	Frew McMillan / Betty Stöve	5	6

COUNTY CHAMPIONSHIP CRICKET WINNERS

The 1979 Schweppes County Championship was the 80th officially organised running of the County Championship and saw Essex win their first ever title.

Pos.	Team	Pld.	W	L	D	Pts.
1	**Essex**	**21**	**13**	**4**	**4**	**281**
2	Worcestershire	21	7	4	10	204
3	Surrey	21	6	3	12	192
4	Sussex	20	6	4	10	184
5	Kent	22	6	3	13	181

TEST SERIES CRICKET

Australia vs England
England win the series 5-1

Test	Dates			Ground	Result
1st Test	1978	1st Dec	6th Dec	The Gabba	England by 7 wickets
2nd Test	1978	15th Dec	20th Dec	WACA Ground	England by 166 runs
3rd Test	1978	29th Dec	3rd Jan	Melbourne Cricket Ground	Australia by 103 runs
4th Test	1979	6th Jan	11th Jan	Sydney Cricket Ground	England by 93 runs
5th Test	1979	27th Jan	1st Feb	Adelaide Oval	England by 205 runs
6th Test	1979	10th Feb	14th Feb	Sydney Cricket Ground	England by 9 wickets

England vs West Indies
England win the series 1-0

Test	Dates			Ground	Result
1st Test	1979	12th Jul	16th Jul	Edgbaston	England by an inns. and 83 runs
2nd Test	1979	2nd Aug	7th Aug	Lord's	Match drawn
3rd Test	1979	16th Aug	21st Aug	Headingley	Match drawn
4th Test	1979	30th Aug	4th Sep	Kennington Oval	Match drawn

Australia vs England
Australia win the series 3-0

Test	Dates			Ground	Result
1st Test	1979	14th Dec	19th Dec	WACA Ground	Australia by 138 runs
2nd Test	1980	4th Jan	8th Jan	Sydney Cricket Ground	Australia by 6 wickets
3rd Test	1980	1st Feb	6th Feb	Melbourne Cricket Ground	Australia by 8 wickets

THE COST OF LIVING

COMPARISON CHART

	1979 Price	1979 Price Today	2018 Price	% Change
3 Bedroom House	£20,000	£109,380	£227,874	+108.3%
Weekly Income	£50	£273.45	£535	+95.6%
Pint Of Beer	68p	£3.72	£3.60	-3.2%
Cheese (lb)	£1.17	£6.40	£3.38	-47.2%
Bacon (lb)	£1.24	£6.78	£3.34	-50.7%
The Beano	6p	33p	£2.50	+657.6%

Checkout the New Year prices

Knorr Packet Soups, makes 1½ pints . **13½p**

Shredded Wheat, pack of 18 .... **28p**

Hartleys Garden Peas, 10oz can........... **9½p**

Hartleys Whole Carrots, 10oz can........... **9½p**

Heinz Spaghetti in Tomato & Cheese Sauce, 15½oz can **14½p**

Heinz Big Soups, 15oz can........ **26p**

Del Monte Tomato Ketchup, 12oz bottle **19½p**

McVities Jamaica Ginger/ Dark Orange/ Lemon Spice Cakes, each...... **23p**

Kit Kat 2 x 11p (flashed Tesco Checkout price) **19p**

Birds Custard, family drum...... **25p**

Sunlight Lemon Liquid (flashed 32p), giant size **27p**

Persil Automatic (flashed 50½p), E3 size......... **44½p**

HEINZ BAKED BEANS **12½p** 15¾oz Can

HEINZ CREAM OF TOMATO SOUP 14¾oz Can **15½p**

JACOB'S Cream Crackers (flashed 15p) 200g Pack **12½p**

Andrex **23½p** Pack of Two

McVITIE'S MILK CHOCOLATE HOME WHEAT 300g Pack **32p**

8½p 5oz Pot

Stork SB margarine 2 x 8oz Pack **29p**

E3 Size (flashed 51½p) **44½p** **Persil**

Kennomeat Dog Food, large can.......... **19p**

Choosy Cat Food, large can.......... **16p**

Stork Packet Margarine, 8oz pack........ **12½p**

Findus Beefburgers, 8oz pack......... **42p**

Findus Cod Fish Fingers, 10oz pack **49p**

New Zealand Leg of Lamb, per lb **98p**

New Zealand Shoulder of Lamb, per lb **62p**

New Zealand Lamb Chops, per lb **96p**
(offers end 6th January 1979)

Large Jaffa Grapefruit, each . **14p**

Class 1 French Golden Delicious Apples (not pre-packed), per lb **14p**
(offers end 6th January 1979)

Checkout at ✓ TESCO

Price cuts that help keep the cost of living in check

Introducing Sainsbury's Discount '79.

It carries on where Discount '78 left off.

Last January, Sainsbury's introduced Discount '78. Overnight, Sainsbury's shoppers felt the benefit of regular savings on the things they had to buy, week after week.

This January, we're going to do exactly the same. With one subtle difference. We've called it Discount '79. It starts this month and carries on till December 31st.

Become a Sainsbury shopper and with Discount '79 you'll always find a good tea and coffee at a heavy discount. You'll always find biscuits, baked beans, margarine, frozen food and breakfast cereals at a heavy discount. And of course you'll always find the quality and freshness you expect from Sainsbury's.

In fact you'll find Sainsbury's Discount '79 every bit as good as Discount '78. Here are just some examples:

Canned Goods

Sainsbury's Beans in Tomato Sauce	15¾oz	11½p
Heinz Baked Beans	15¾oz	13p
Heinz Soups	14¾oz	15½p
Crosse & Blackwell Spaghetti	15oz	14½p
Lych-Gate Tomatoes	14oz	13p
Sainsbury's Garden Peas	19oz	17p
Batchelors Bigga Proc. Peas	10oz	9p
S & B Corned Beef	12oz	48½p
Walls Stewed Steak	15oz	55p
Heinz Rice Pudding	15½oz	14p
Heinz Sponge Puddings	10½oz	26p
S & B Marmalade	1lb	23p
Whiskas Cat Food	13.6oz	25½p

Fresh & Frozen Food

Dutch Edam	per lb	58p
Sainsbury's Fruit Yogurt	150g	8½p
Sainsbury's Green Label Margarine	1lb	26p
Danelard	½lb	9½p
Roasting Chicken	per lb from	42p
Sainsbury's Beefburgers (Frozen)	4's	36p
Birds Eye Cod Fish Fingers	10's	49p
Birds Eye Chicken Pie	Ind.	23p

Household & Toiletries

Palmolive Washing-Up Liquid (7p off pack)	19fl.oz	27p
Bold (50½p priced pack)	E3	45p
Ariel (52½p priced pack)	E3	46½p
Persil Auto (£1.65 priced pack)	E10	£1.48
Comfort Fabric Conditioner (40p priced pack)	994ml	36p
Colgate Toothpaste	50ml	22½p
Fairy Toilet Soap	142g	12½p
Head & Shoulders Lotion Shampoo	100g	33p
Tampax Super	x 40	75p
Albor Toilet Tissue	2 rolls	18½p

Off Licence

Double Century Sherries		£1.55
Sainsbury's Yugoslav Laski Riesling	1 litre	£1.55
Sainsbury's Italian Vermouth	1 litre	£1.59

Groceries

Sainsbury's Red Label Tea	¼lb	17½p	McDougalls Flour Plain/SR	1½ kilo	31½p
PG Tips Tea Bags	8oz	49p	Oxo Cubes	12's	17p
Sainsbury's Instant Coffee Powder refill	4oz	64p	Sainsbury's Vegetable Oil	1 litre	54p
Horlicks	16oz	56p	Sainsbury's Caster Sugar	1 kilo	35p
Sainsbury's Porridge Oats	1 kilo	32p	McVitie's Chocolate Homewheat	200g	24p
Kellogg's Corn Flakes	500g	32½p	Sainsbury's Digestive	200g	12p
Sainsbury's Cornflakes	500g	28½p	Jacob's Club	x 5	21½p
Heinz Tomato Ketchup	20oz	38p	Jacob's Cream Crackers	200g	13½p
Heinz Ploughman's Pickle	10½oz	25p	Sainsbury's Lemonade	1 litre	19½p
			Sainsbury's Packet Soups	1½pt. equiv.	11½p

All offers subject to availability

Good food still costs less at Sainsbury's.

CLOTHES

Fur Fabric Coat	£29
Full Length Quilted Nylon Winter Coat	£14.05
Cotton Cord Bomber Jacket	£10.99
Anorak	£8.49
Tailored Blazer	£17.49
English Lady Evening Dress	£14.95
Shirtwaister Dress	£8.75
Zipper Cardigan	£5.99
Turtle Neck Pullover	£3.25
Fancy Print Shirt	£2.99
Foster's Fashion Trousers	£6.99
Western Style Indigo Jeans	£5.99
Blue Denim Jeans	£3.79
Brushed Cotton Pyjamas	£4.75
Wolsey Briefs (3 pack)	£2.45
Woolworth's One-Piece Swimming Costume	£2.99
Plain Coloured Socks (3 pack)	69p

TOYS

2-Wheel Pavement Cycle With Stabilisers	£22.95
Giant Ride-On Dumper Truck	£26.95
Pedal-Drive Go-Kart	£22.95
Wendy Playhouse	£7.95
Trudy Continental Dolls Pushchair	£4.95
Superjouet Full Size Table Football	£9.95
Electronic Reed Organ	£19.95
Acoustic Wooden Folk Guitar	£14.95
Battery Operated Train Set	£6.75
Play Family Dolls House	£13.95
Music Box Record Player	£8.95
Circus Train	£10.95
Wooden Desk & Stool	£17.95
Fisher-Price Activity Centre	£7.95
Junior Tool Set	£7.95

ELECTRICAL ITEMS

Ferguson 20in Colour TV	£254.95
Philips 14in Mono Portable TV	£82.95
Ferguson Videostar Video Recorder	£589.95
Pilot Stereo Music Centre	£114.95
Bush Radio Cassette	£37.95
Hotpoint Automatic Washing Machine	£149.95
Creda Tumble Dryer	£72.95
Indesit Dishwasher	£148.95
Zanussi 6.7/5.1 Cu.ft. Fridge Freezer	£194.95
Electrolux Vacuum Cleaner	£36.50
Binatone Clock Radio	£23.95
Kenwood Chef	£61.95
Morphy Richards Toaster	£16.50
Moulinex Hairdryer	£5.75
Goblin Teasmade	£31.95
Astral Dry Iron	£6.95
Northern Electric Overblanket	£22.95
Black & Decker Single Speed Drill	£16.95

OTHER PRICES

Ford Cortina Mark V 1.3l	£3,475
Peugeot 305GL	£3,365
Fiat Strada	£3,044
Ford Fiesta	£2,260
Skoda 105S	£1,850
12V Car Battery	from £11.95
Quantas Return Flight To Sydney, Australia	from £334
New York 7 Day Holiday	£220
London To Paris - Train & Ship (night / day fares)	£26 / £38
Malaga Glass Top Dining Set + 4 Chairs	£49.95
Berkeley Three-Piece Suite	£279.95
Silentnight 4ft 6in Midnight Divan Set	£95.95
Senator Teak Effect Wall Unit	£89.95
Quality Axminster Carpet (per sq. yard)	£7.75
Set Of 7 Jaguar Golf Clubs	£44.95
Folding Golf Trolley	£12.95
Zig Zag Sewing Machine	£59.95
Rollei Sound Cine Camera	£199.95
Olympus OM-1 Camera	£179
Polaroid 10 Instant Camera	£14.50
Ultraview 7x50 Binoculars	£38.50
Odyssey Electronic Watch With LCD Display	£8.95
LP Record	£4.50
Guinness Book Of Records	£4.25
Benson & Hedges Mellow Virginia Tobacco (25g)	73p
TV Times Magazine	13p

65

The new Ford Cortina

Ford introduce important engineering advances into a car that's built for reliability

Listen, if we are going to leave any oil for our kids,

It has no sexy bulges.

No chrome embellishments.

They cause drag and waste fuel.

True, the Strada may seem a bit stark without them.

But it's also highly aerodynamic without them.

So streamlined, in fact, that it actually gives more mpg than many smaller cars.

And more room inside than much bigger saloons.

You've heard this before? So had we. And we remember curling our lips when the computer said it was possible.

But look at the figures:

The Strada has as much front legroom as a Jaguar XJ5.3.

Slightly more rear legroom than a Peugeot 504.

And considerably more rear headroom than a Mercedes 450SEL.

As for the fuel consumption, well, let's have a few more facts.

You have a choice of two engine sizes. The Strada 65 CL has a 1300cc unit that gives 42.2mpg.*

(Better than the Escort 1.3 and the Chevette hatchback.)

The Strada 75 CL has a 1500cc engine that gives 43.7mpg.*

(Better than the Allegro and the Golf GLS.)

This, we might add, without sacrificing the sparkle people expect from a Fiat. The cars have top speeds of 93 and 99mph respectively. This may not be enough for you, we know that.

Perhaps you yearn for a multicylinder, fuel guzzling, scarlet monster?

As Italians we understand that particular lust only too well.

But just try repeating this to yourself a couple of times before bed:

The last oil well runs dry in forty years time.

The last oil well runs dry in forty years time.

In the cold light of day the *FIAT* Strada will seem an exceptionally beautiful motor car.

The Strada.

more cars have got to look like this.

66

CARTOONS

Printed in Great Britain
by Amazon